TEN COMMANDMENTS OF LOVE

© All rights reserved. This book or parts thereof may not be reproduced in any form, stored in any retrieval system, or transmitted in any form by any means—electronic, mechanical, photocopy, recording, or otherwise—without prior written permission of the publisher, except as provided by United States of America copyright law. For permission requests, write to the publisher, at "Attention: Permissions Coordinator," at the address below. Nathan E. Austin Ministries 1525 NW 7th Street Pompano Beach FL. 33069

Published by:
Nathan E. Austin Ministries
1525 NW 7th Street
Pompano Beach, FL. 33069

Disclaimer

I believe in the sanctity of marriage between a man and a woman. I believe the principles discussed in this book become more powerful when applying them as a married couple. However, it has been my desire to write this book for those who are not only MARRIED, but for those who are ENGAGED, COURTING, DATING, LIVING TOGETHER, OR THINKING ABOUT IT. I have used terms such as **spouse, mate, partner, couple** and **significant other** to define relationships. As a result of reading this book, my prayer is that you and the one you love be drawn closer together in Jesus Name. Amen!
— **Pastor Nathan E. Austin**

Table of Contents

ACKNOWLEDGMENTS 5

INTRODUCTION
It's Not Luck! 7

THE FIRST COMMANDMENT OF LOVE:
Exclusivity 11

THE SECOND COMMANDMENT OF LOVE:
Thou Shall Not Substitute 17

THE THIRD COMMANDMENT OF LOVE:
Speak Well of Your Mate 21

THE FOURTH COMMANDMENT OF LOVE:
Remember The Sabbath 27

THE FIFTH COMMANDMENT OF LOVE:
Honor Your Spouse by Showing Gratitude 33

THE SIXTH COMMANDMENT OF LOVE:
Thou Shall Not Kill 41

THE SEVENTH COMMANDMENT OF LOVE:
Thou Shall Not Cheat 47

THE EIGHTH COMMANDMENT OF LOVE:
Be a Person of Integrity 57

THE NINTH COMMANDMENT OF LOVE:
Be Truthful 61

THE TENTH COMMANDMENT OF LOVE:
Be Content with What You Have 65

ACKNOWLEDGMENTS

Life is a team sport. You cannot go very far working alone. I have been blessed to surround myself with a group of people who have supported, encouraged, inspired and challenged me to be great.

To my wife Kimberly Austin: My life has never been the same since you stepped into it. God has given me great ideas, but they would all be stuck in my mind if you had not come along to put them in motion. Thank you for helping me publish my first literary work! We partnered together in 2016 to present this idea to our church. Who would have known that 365 days later, we would present it to the world? I am forever blessed to have you in my life. Thank you for being there every step of the way. Our relationship will now be a model for other couples to live by. To God Be The Glory for the great things He has done and will continue to do through us!

To my sons Noah and Joshua: You are too young now to appreciate what your father has accomplished. I pray that when you are old enough to find love like the love I've found with your mother, this book will help you keep these Love Commandments.

To my family: You have always believed in the plan God has for my life. Thank you for raising me to fear God and serve him at an early age. You have always supported me in whatever I have done, and because of this, I am able to be everything God has called me to be.

To The Zion Church: This book is a direct result of you. I often remind you that as much as you think you need me, I need you even more. You have allowed me to work outside of the box. You have pushed me to be the pastor and now author God has called me to be. You were my "guinea pigs" for this project. Your positive feedback has made this work possible. Thank you for giving me time to birth this book. Your confidence in me has allowed me to Position God's People to Prosper!

To my editor Aubrey Grant: Thank you for your time and commitment to making sure this book was produced in the spirit of excellence. I look forward to working with you on future literary projects.

Finally to the Band of Brothers (The Austins, Stanleys, and McDuffies): I look forward to discussing this book during our "June Wedding Anniversary Celebrations." It's not often that three young African Americans find LOVE and keep it for as long as we have. May God continue to bless each of our relationships and our children as we strive to be role models for them.

INTRODUCTION

It's Not Luck!

Good relationships and marriages don't just happen. I've heard people say on many occasions, "Man, you are lucky to have a woman like her." Or, "You hit the relationship lotto when you found them!" Now don't get me wrong, I know I'm blessed to have the wife that I have. However, luck had nothing to do with it. From the time I got to know my wife as a friend, I told her she would be my wife.

Now I must admit I was not ready for a wife at that time, but I knew deep down I wanted nobody but her. You see, I believe you don't just hook up with the right person and get lucky. Why not? Because good relationships aren't just about two people coming together. They aren't built on passion either. Good relationships are built on principle.

In Scripture, we find the best guidelines and principles for healthy loving relationships. One of the things I love about God's Word is unlike other books, **it's never outdated**! The Bible is just as applicable today as it was to the ancient Jews living in Israel.

One of the most ancient Scriptures with which we are familiar is the Ten Commandments. These commandments were written as principles that God wanted us to live by. By now, I know what you are thinking: "What in the world does the Ten Commandments have to do with creating a great relationship?"

First let me give you these Commandments that can be found in Exodus 20. Take a few moments to read them carefully.

I. *You shall have no other gods before Me.*
II. *You shall not make for yourself a carved image...*
III. *You shall not take the name of the LORD your God in vain...*
IV. *Remember the Sabbath day, to keep it holy.*
V. *Honor your father and your mother, that your days may be long upon the land which the LORD your God is giving you.*
VI. *You shall not murder.*
VII. *You shall not commit adultery.*
VIII. *You shall not steal.*
IX. *You shall not bear false witness against your neighbor.*
X. *You shall not covet your neighbor's house; you shall not covet your neighbor's wife, nor his male servant, nor his female servant, nor his ox, nor his donkey, nor anything that is your neighbor's.*

Now let's begin this journey and see exactly how God has lead me to share with you "The Ten Commandments of Love." After reading each commandment you will discover there are questions or sections entitled "Let's Talk." These sections are designed for you and your mate to discuss the questions that have been presented. These exercises will allow both of you to determine exactly where you are and how to get where you need to go. I pray this book helps you to become the **Power Couple** God has designed for you to be.

THE FIRST COMMANDMENT OF LOVE:

Exclusivity

The first of the Ten Commandments is simply this, as found in Exodus 20:3, "You shall have no other gods before Me."

Interpretation: Thou Shall Be Exclusive.

What is God saying in this commandment?
He wants to have an exclusive relationship with you. He wants to be your one and only. He will not settle for being your flavor of the month.

This is appropriate in marriage as well. We are to have an exclusive relationship with our spouse. It's been said that Henry Ford was asked on his golden anniversary (fifty years of marriage), "What's the secret of your success in marriage?" He said, "The secret of my successful marriage is the same secret that I have in business - I stick to the same model." In traditional wedding vows, the man and woman pledge their devotion until death parts them. In relationships, there should be no competition. My wife has no competition.

I am not shopping for a new model.

She won't have to worry about me having a mid-life crisis.

She won't have to worry about me trying to get an upgrade or trading in the old model.

I will not be shopping in the future. *One is all I need.*

Her age won't have any effect on my attraction to her.

It amazes me how some men are drawn to beautiful younger women as if they have not aged themselves. Remember just like you can find someone younger, perkier and slimmer, she can find someone longer, stronger and faster. Married people or those in a committed relationship should not need an office spouse, a side person, a secret lover, or confidant. When you commit, what you are saying is you are putting all your eggs in one basket. It's all or nothing; if it does not work, you do not have a **Plan B** option.

Nobody is coming off the bench! Nobody is warming up! Nobody is waiting in the bullpen! You are either going to win together or lose together.

When God made man, He said it is good. But then He said, "It is not good that he is alone. I am going to make a helper suitable for him." Then the Bible says God took one of Adam's ribs, and He formed a woman named Eve and brought her to the man. God did not take four or five ribs and say, "Okay, Adam, here is Eve, and here is Lois, and here is Samantha, and here is Rachel." No, it was just one.

In order to have a healthy relationship, you have to be committed for life. An exclusive relationship means that you are no longer shopping, not even window-shopping. To quote the late Michael Jackson, "**THIS IS IT!**" If you're considering marriage and are not willing to obey this commandment, **SEPARATE NOW!** Don't waste each other's time for another second.

Let's Talk It OUT

Who is presently the person that can unconscionably come before your significant other?
(including parents, friends and even children)

_____
_____
_____
_____
_____
_____
_____
_____
_____
_____
_____
_____
_____
_____
_____

How committed are you to your relationship?

What has been your secret to success in your relationship?

TEN COMMANDMENTS OF LOVE

THE SECOND COMMANDMENT OF LOVE:

Thou Shall Not Substitute

In the Second Commandment recorded in Exodus 20:4-6, we are given the second principle for a strong marriage: *"You shall not make for yourself a carved image—any likeness of anything that is in heaven above, or that is in the earth beneath, or that is in the water under the earth; you shall not bow down to them nor serve them. For I, the LORD your God, am a jealous God."*

Interpretation: Thou Shall Not Substitute

God commanded that we not worship carved images, whether in heaven, on earth, or in the sea. He wanted to make sure everything was covered. God said, "Do not make images of Me and then worship them. Do not love or worship a substitute for Me. Love Me."

Some religions have made pictures, statues, and idols and then called them holy. They are all imitations. They are all substitutes. *In marriage there are no substitutes.*

This commandment may sound a lot like the first, so allow me to explain the difference. My wife and I are huge sports fans. After watching numerous of hours of team sports over the years, we've learned about one thing: *the art of substitution.*

Every team has a group of players they call "The Starters". However, they have other players on their roster who are also capable of playing well, they're just not starters. In sports many of these players are known as specialists or situational players. This means they are on the team because they fit certain game time situations. These players are just as important to the team as the starters because as good as the starters are, they can't play the entire game. They will get tired, and when they do, the coach will have to sit them down to take a breather. Once they have caught their breath they can come right back in the game. Until then, the coach must substitute them by utilizing the other players on the roster that best fit the game time situation. These substitutions happen throughout the game until the game is completed. Wow, that's a lot of substitution!

Just in case you don't know by now, a relationship is not a game. **It is serious**! It's not a competition. You won't always get the outcome you expect, but that's ok! What you must understand is, when things are not going picture perfect in your relationship, you cannot look for fulfillment in some other person or in some other thing. That's why **exclusivity** is so important. People tend to value what they have when they have no other options. Unlike team sports, you cannot resort to using a sub.

Beware of Imitations!

Here's another reason this commandment is different. God realized his people were starting to create cheap carbon copies of Him. They were not putting them before God, they were treating them as Gods.

This can happen in a relationship as well, not just with flesh and blood but other things as well. Notice God specifically used the word images - wow, it's like he wrote these words yesterday. Oh, how the world today controls our mind through images. So much so that people are now finding fulfillment from images such as pornography and other graphic images. Graphic images are so powerful there's a term in marketing called "sex sells." So if sex images can persuade you to buy a product, don't you think they can persuade you to do something else? **Pornography is a substitute image!**

When a man or woman watches pornography, they are watching a substitute. In their mind they are fantasizing that what they are watching is really happening to them. They are directing their passion and sexuality toward those images. This is a substitute. Therefore, they are robbing their mate of that intimacy.

When a women indulges herself in other outside activities, or even friends that prevent her from spending anytime with her mate, that is a substitute. Substitutes can never take the place of the *Real Thing*; they are lesser ingredients, or cheaper versions. I will explain in Chapter Seven how substitution can ruin a relationship.

Do not allow any substitute, no matter what it might be, to take the place of intimacy with your spouse.

Let's Talk It OUT

What can you do to assure your partner that your relationship is a priority and that there are "NO SUBSTITUTES"?

_____
_____
_____
_____
_____
_____
_____
_____
_____
_____
_____
_____
_____
_____

Who or what has been a substitute for intimacy in your relationship?

_____
_____
_____
_____
_____
_____
_____
_____

THE THIRD COMMANDMENT OF LOVE:

Speak Well of Your Mate

Exodus 20:7 gives us our Third Commandment of marriage: "You shall not take the name of the LORD your God in vain, for the LORD will not hold him guiltless who takes His name in vain."

Interpretation: Thou Shall Build Up and not tear down.

Many misunderstand the term "in vain." It means empty, meaningless, insincere, not showing due respect. When we speak flippantly, shallowly, or lightly about someone, we erode our respect for that person. Some people are just far too casual in the way they speak of their spouse, and it erodes their respect for him or her. Few things can affect a relationship more than words. Words are containers. They can contain love, hate, joy, or even bitterness.

The Book of James says that our tongue is like a rudder on a ship. It will send the ship of your relationship in whatever direction your words go. Some people are on the brink of divorce because they talk about divorce. Just listen to the words they say. Are they negative or positive? Are they critical or encouraging? There's a scripture that says, "Out of the abundance of the heart, the mouth speaks."

If you examine that scripture, it simply means that whatever is in your heart will come out of your month. What should always be in your heart are words of encouragement. There's another scripture I like in the Book of Ephesians that says, "Let no corrupting talk come out of your mouths, but only such as is good for building up, as fits the occasion, that it may give grace to those who hear."

My wife and I work in a profession that is filled with negativity. No matter what we do or how hard we try, someone always tries to tear us down. Therefore we've discovered that the world has enough people tearing us down. We cannot add to the destruction; we must be a part of the building up process.

Be the first to build

I spoke earlier about office romance. Do you wonder how most office romances get started? Someone on the job is telling your partner things that you should be telling them. Believe it or not, the work place is a place where a lot of communication happens.

A lot of times, your spouse may leave the house feeling down. They feel down about how they look, down about not getting something accomplished, or down for various other reasons. You are the first person to see them in the morning - if you don't build them up then who will? I'll tell you who: a co-worker or a close friend with whom they may communicate with throughout the day.

We often take communication with our partners for granted and when we do, someone is always waiting to pick up the pieces. Only single people should have to encourage themselves. When you have a partner, they should never let someone else build them up before you. While you can't control what others may say to them,

NOBODY should outdo YOU when it comes to building up your mate. There's a lot of talk in our country now about building walls.

I encourage you to build a wall of encouragement around your spouse so tall that the highest amount of discouragement will not affect them.

In the future, think about what you say. Are you building up your partner with your words? Learn to speak well of your mate. Be lavish with your praise. You will be pleased with where those words will take your relationship.

Reference Reading
Luke 6.45 NKJ
James 3:2-6 NLT
Ephesians 4.29 NLT

Let's Talk It OUT

On a scale from 1 to 10 how good are you at communication? Which areas could you improve?

_____
_____
_____
_____
_____
_____
_____
_____

___

How often do you and your partner share your feelings with one another?

___

How well are you at discerning how your mate is feeling each day?

___

TEN COMMANDMENTS OF LOVE

What types of words or things do you use to build up your partner?

TEN COMMANDMENTS OF LOVE

THE FOURTH COMMANDMENT OF LOVE:

Remember The Sabbath

The Fourth Commandment, found in Exodus 20:8-11:
Remember the Sabbath day, to keep it holy. Six days you shall labor and do all your work, but the seventh day is the Sabbath of the LORD your God. In it you shall do no work: you, nor your son, nor your daughter, nor your male servant, nor your female servant, nor your cattle, nor your stranger who is within your gates. For in six days the LORD made the heavens and the earth, the sea, and all that is in them, and rested the seventh day. Therefore the LORD blessed the Sabbath day and hallowed it.

Interpretation: Thou Shall Spend Quality Time Together

Sabbath means an intermission. It means to put down your work and rest. Take a break! Holy means dedicated or consecrated to the Lord. "If you want a long-term relationship with Me," God says, "We have to have time together. I want special time, exclusive time. I want a whole day." In the same way, in order to have a healthy relationship, both parties need time together - special time, exclusive time, sometimes extravagant time. In many cases we all know that if we do not schedule it, it won't happen. When preparing to write this book, I did a little research. I found that surveys show the average couple spends thirty-seven minutes or less in face-to-face conversation every week. Please understand that this was a survey polling couples ages forty-five and up. I bet before you were married or got serious, you spent a lot more time together in a week, didn't you? Now take into account that we are in a new social media, technological era. A world filled with cell phones and ipads. These devices serve as major distractions and may soon ruin communication as we know it. If your relationship is to thrive, you need to spend exclusive time together. You can't build a relationship and not spend time together. It is just not possible. Exclusive time is quality time. Kim and I have extremely busy schedules:

We lead our church as Pastor and First Lady.
We lead our community development corporations
We lead our for-profit enterprise
We have our own private business

Not to mention raising two extremely active young men.

Needless to say, we don't have a large quantity of free time. However, we have made it our mission to maintain **Quality Time** with each other. Working together in so many areas can be a blessing and a burden for us. It's a blessing because we do spend a lot time together; however it's also a burden because most of our time together, we are discussing or performing business. Nevertheless, we still have to find time where it's ALL ABOUT US. Not about our church, business, or even our children. The strength of our relationship demands it.

Balancing The Unbalanced

I used to stress about trying to balance all the things I have to do while maintaining **Quality Time** with my wife. I learned that I will never find balance. Having balance means being equal on both sides. For us, that's unrealistic. However, what we can do is when we find ourselves getting too far off balance, we can cut back on something else until we feel some sense of balance again. So now I place my wife on my calendar just as I would anything else. Yes she's on my CALENDAR. Anything that's important to me, that requires my direct attention, I place on my calendar. So if it's not on my calendar that means it's not important. After more than fifteen years of being together, she should not have to fight for my attention. As a matter of fact, every now and then, I squeeze her in when I have slow moments in my day (If you know what I mean!). Just like the Sabbath, there has to be certain times during the week, month, and year that are "HOLY." This means no one can interrupt those moments -, not the TV, phone, tablet, nothing! Check out this little statement I wrote to my church a few years ago.

This Is A Phone

It Doesn't……
- Call you when you are in Stranded
- Care for you when you are Sick
- **Console you when you are Sad**
- Celebrate your Success
- **Correct you when you Sin**
- Carry you when you are Stuck
- **Comfort you in a Storm**

But we say we can't live without it

You know who does all these things? A Good Partner! Stop what you are doing right now and give someone you love a hug. Let them know this phone will not ruin your partnership. Time is too precious to waste!!!
© Nathan E. Austin Ministries

#cherishthethingsthatareirreplaceable

NATHAN E. AUSTIN
MINISTRIES

As I grow older, I understand how precious time really is. Don't waste it all doing things that don't bring value to your life or relationship. If you are a young couple and you don't have children, by all means live it up with your mate. Trust me, those years go by fast. Before we had kids we booked cruises every year, sometimes twice a year. We attended several sporting events. We went to South Beach and just hung out with each other. Now that we have kids, we don't do any of these things as much, but we still TAKE TIME for each other. Notice I said TAKE TIME and not MAKE TIME. We have discovered trying to make time to do things hardly ever works. Therefore we have to TAKE IT, even at the expense of something else that might be important. It helps that we like to do the same types of things, so when we do hang out, it's always a blast. I believe compatibility has helped us maintain this commandment.

Let's Talk It OUT

How much time do you spend together every week?

_____
_____
_____
_____
_____
_____
_____
_____
_____
_____
_____
_____

TEN COMMANDMENTS OF LOVE

What are some of the things you use to do before you got married?

_____
_____
_____
_____
_____
_____
_____
_____
_____
_____
_____
_____
_____

Who or what has stopped you from spending quality time together?

_____
_____
_____
_____
_____
_____
_____
_____
_____
_____
_____
_____

TEN COMMANDMENTS OF LOVE

THE FIFTH COMMANDMENT OF LOVE:

Honor Your Spouse by Showing Gratitude

The Fifth Commandment gives us our next principle for a healthy and vibrant marriage. It is found in Exodus 20:12. "Honor your father and your mother, that your days may be long upon the land which the LORD your God is giving you."

Interpretation: Thou Shall Show Gratitude.

You can easily rewrite the verse by saying, "Honor your spouse, that your marriage may be long upon the land which the LORD your God is giving you."

Among other things, God is saying we must be grateful. Generally, parents spend a lot of time, labor, and money, sometimes to the point of radical sacrifice, just to give their kids an edge in life. One of the most tragic things you could ever see is an ungrateful or unthankful child. William Shakespeare said, "How sharper than a serpent's tooth it is to have a thankless child." It is very difficult to have a relationship with an ungrateful or selfish person. "Thank you" is an important phrase to your parents, and an extremely important phrase in relationships. It is difficult to live with someone who takes you and all of your efforts for granted by not showing gratitude.

The original wording of this commandment is a segue into how you build a successful relationship. How a person treats their parents is a sign of how they will treat you. If they honor their parents, more than likely they will honor you. If they disrespect their parents, they will probably disrespect you. Whether you are a man or woman, don't ever forget that you are a gift from God. (James 1:7)

Appreciating Your Gift

As I mentioned in my intro, I don't think great relationships are built when people just "hook up." Call me old fashioned, but I still believe a man and a woman are a gift to each other. According to Proverbs 18.22, "He who finds a wife finds a good thing, and obtains favor from the LORD" (NKJ). The word "find" brings along the thought that man was searching for the right woman and was blessed to find her. Therefore, that makes that woman "God sent." The same thought applies for a woman; God allowed the perfect man to find her. We all learned as children that when you receive a gift, you must show how grateful you are to have it. Your gratitude is not just shown to the person who gave you the gift, but to the gift itself. That means we must spend a significant amount of time showing our mate just how grateful we are to have him or her in our lives.

You may be thinking, "I don't say it, but I am grateful in my heart. I truly am!" Well, hooray for you. You are blessed because in your heart, you know you are grateful. However, it does your partner no good if you do not vocalize your gratitude. If you fail to demonstrate your gratitude, I doubt that you are truly grateful because Jesus said, "Out of the abundance of the heart the mouth speaks" (Luke 6.45). If it is not being expressed, then chances are, it is not truly there. Maybe you think you don't have a lot for which to be grateful. But there must be something for which you can say thank you, something for which you can praise your mate. Look for those things, and accentuate the positive. Men, if you have kids, I'm sure you can think about how much time your sweetheart spends with them. Every night, my wife spends time helping with homework, cooking dinner, bathing our kids, ironing their clothes, etc. Truly, this is something to be thankful for. Ladies, think about how hard your man works to take care of the needs of the house. Isn't that enough to say thank you?

How Can I Say Thank You?

You may be wondering, "How can I say thank you?" Well, these are just a few suggestions.

1. **Take on a task.**
If your spouse is the one who cooks, cleans, and takes care of the kids, try taking on that responsibility for a day or two. Slip them a note that says, "Take the day off!"

2. **Give them a "Me Day" Ticket.**
Find some things where they can be the center of attention: a day of golf, a spa treatment, or a day at the mall. Get them out of their everyday atmosphere so they can spend some time alone doing what makes them happy. Being in relationship is about partnership, however time ALONE is still important. Of course, hanging out with you and the kids is great, but you never want your partner to lose their sense of self.

3. Just say it.
You will be surprised how powerful the words "thank you" can be. A random thank you is really not random, considering the fact that your mate does something worth being thankful for everyday. However, because it is unexpected it will make them feel so appreciated and probably push them to go the extra mile.

4. Express it to others.
We live in a time that is dominated by social media. The power of social media is that it gives people the opportunity to broadcast anything to the entire world. You may ask, "Why is social media important?" Notice I used the word broadcast. When you tell your partner something in person, although it's very meaningful, you are narrowcasting your sentiments. Narrowcasting means your audience is very small. However, social media platforms allow you to broadcast to everyone that you truly love your mate. Trust me, when they see you are not afraid to tell everybody how you feel about them, it provides a sense of love that cannot be measured.

Let's think about Valentine's Day. Every year stores make millions of dollars on people who want to broadcast their love. It's funny because the same flowers, cards, candy, and teddy bears are drastically marked down one day later. I mean, they are almost giving the stuff away. Let's not talk about the restaurants. We've all waited hours to eat at a place that you can go to the next day and a pick any seat. Why? Because the world likes to brag on this one day. I'm the type of person who likes to stand out. I like being different. Therefore, I tend to do things on days that are significant to my relationship, such as celebrating a first date, wedding anniversary, birthday, or any special moment in time. The benefits of this are:

- Things are less expensive
- Places are not crowded
- She knows I really thought about her
- I stand out more when I share these things on social media

Yes, you stand out more when you don't do things with the crowd. Therefore, you receive more recognition. When everyone else is complimenting what you are doing, trust me, you will receive **BROWNIE POINTS!** So do yourself a favor and take time out right now to express your gratitude, whether it's through an action, a card, or words. **Your mate might just thank you later! (If you know what I mean).**

Let's Talk It Out

When was the last time you verbalized your gratitude?
_____
_____
_____
_____
_____
_____
_____
_____
_____
_____
_____
_____
_____

Other than "Broadcast Holidays," can you think of other times you might express your gratitude towards your mate?

-Besides tangible things, what are some things you can do to show your mate just how much you appreciate them?

TEN COMMANDMENTS OF LOVE

THE SIXTH COMMANDMENT OF LOVE:

Thou Shall Not Kill

The Sixth Commandment God gave to Israel in Exodus 20:13 was, "You shall not murder."

Interpretation: Thou Shall Not Kill Your Relationship.

While you might think this commandment is not too applicable, I believe it is crucial to the success of your relationship. It is telling you not to destroy your partner! Jesus helps us understand this principle in Matthew 5:21-22. He said, "You have heard that it was said to those of old, 'You shall not murder, and whoever murders will be in danger of the judgment.' But I say to you that whoever is angry with his brother without a cause shall be in danger of the judgment." Jesus went right to the root of murder: anger and hatred. If you are going to have a good, healthy, lasting relationship, you need to learn to be gentle. People who are easily angered, who are violent or have an explosive temper, destroy relationships.

Adhere to the Warning Signs

If you are dating someone who blows up easily, you ought to take this as a warning sign. If they get mad about things at the drop of a hat, that anger can be turned on you very easily. You might want to address anger issues before getting heavily involved in a relationship. Ask any police officer, the absolute worst call they respond to is a domestic call. That's because things tend to turn ugly very quickly. Two people can love each other one minute, hate each other the next, and then go right back to loving each other. Just as that statement seemed like a rollercoaster (up and down), so will your relationship. Unaddressed anger is like a ticking time bomb waiting to explode at any second.

Anger erodes relationships. If you have a hot temper, get it under control, or the devil will control you through it.

Another way anger is expressed is by going stone cold (using silence) and angry moves to punish your mate. This is not healthy for a relationship. If you anger quickly and forgive slowly, you are a hard person to get along with. Work at being quick to forgive, and make the controlling of your anger a serious matter of prayer. God will help you. If you do not master your temper, then it will master you. A bad temper will not only decay and destroy a relationship, it will harm every other meaningful relationship you have in life.

There's Power In Our Words

We've all heard the statement "Sticks and stones may break my bones but word will never hurt me." Well this statement is probably more accurate: "Sticks and stones may break my bones but words can kill me." There's a Proverbs scripture that says: "Death and life are in the power of the tongue, and they that love it shall eat the fruit thereof." Those words cannot be any more accurate.

You see, when you are in a relationship, the person you are with has a heavy influence on your life. You trust what they have to say and you value their opinion of you. Believe it or not, that's **POWERFUL.** So when your mate says something that hurts you, those words have far more impact than words from an enemy.

That's why anger has to be controlled, because just like the drunk man, the angry man tells no tales. Once you have placed something on the record (by speaking it), it cannot be erased. I've discovered people become very petty when they are in an argument. They will stoop very low in order to win. They intentionally say things that will hurt the other person just to make themselves seem bigger. Let me ask you a question. Is winning one round worth you losing the entire fight? Marriage is a fight I want to win. So sometimes taking a loss in one argument will help me maintain what I have. When you murder your mate with your words, you run the risk of losing them permanently. Stop and ask yourself, will this be worth it?

Choose Life

Let's not just focus on the death portion of this passage. Just like the wrong words can lead to death, the right words can bring about life. As we've already mentioned "Words are a power weapon." I believe it's not just what you say, but how you say it.

My wife, without a doubt, has the most influence over me. She knows me, she thinks like me, she responds like me. I can't tell you how many times she has brought me back to life with her words. During times when I've been depressed due to a failure, she reminded me of my previous success. During times when I thought I didn't preach well, she told me how people shared with her how the message impacted their lives. When I don't think I'm doing a great job at fatherhood, she reminds me how my boys can't function without me. When I don't think I'm a great husband, she lets me know that she can't imagine life with anyone else.

You see, at the time all my statements may seem true, but in a good relationship you don't kick a person while they're down. You use your words to pick them back up. That's what I call speaking life to a dead situation. That's what couples do for each other: they choose "LIFE." So today I command you to choose "LIFE" because death is a painful pill to swallow.

Questions

How well do you use your words?

_____
_____
_____
_____
_____
_____
_____
_____
_____
_____
_____
_____
_____
_____
_____
_____

How well do you mange when you are angry?

How often do you stop and think about your words or thoughts before you communicate them to your mate?

TEN COMMANDMENTS OF LOVE

THE SEVENTH COMMANDMENT OF LOVE

Thou Shall Not Cheat

The Seventh Commandment of love brings us to one of the most vital principles of having the marriage God intends. Exodus 20:14 simply says, "Thou Shall Not Commit Adultery."

No interpretation needed

Caution this will be the longest chapter!!!

In a relationship, you would be hard pressed to imagine anything more damaging than your spouse being unfaithful.

Having a lustful, exploitive disposition has no place. Love gives; lust takes. Love serves; lust demands. Love nourishes; lust chokes. What a wonderful gift God has given us in this thing called sex. It was His idea. It is just as holy as when you lift your hands in church to worship Him. It is God's idea within the context and the confines of marriage. It should be enjoyed. But lust has no place in marriage. It is a poison that will destroy the fabric of your relationship with your spouse.

Faithful In Action and In Thought

Jesus expanded on this idea in Matthew 5, and I want you to read these words very carefully. He said, "You have heard that it was said to those of old, 'You shall not commit adultery.' But I say to you that whoever looks at a woman to lust for her has already committed adultery with her in his heart."

As stated earlier, do not even entertain the thought of allowing pornography into your life. It can destroy your marriage. You are committing heart-adultery when you look at pornographic images and lust after another woman. Do not let the devil have that ground in your heart and life. As this is such a vital command, we are going to stay on this subject a little longer. The question is, how can you affair-proof your relationship, if there is such a thing? I believe you can do it by doing at least three of these things.

1. Affair-Proof Your Relationship with Positive Affirmation

The first way to affair-proof your marriage is to season your marriage with affirming communication.

In Song of Solomon 7:1-6 we read of how Solomon affirmed his bride:

How beautiful are your feet in sandals, O prince's daughter! The curves of your thighs are like jewels, the work of the hands of a skillful workman. Your navel is a rounded goblet; it lacks no blended beverage. Your waist is a heap of wheat set about with lilies. Your two breasts are like two fawns, twins of a gazelle. Your neck is like an ivory tower; your eyes like the pools in Heshbon by the gate of Bath Rabbim. Your nose is like the tower of Lebanon which looks toward Damascus. Your head crowns you like Mount Carmel, and the hair of your head is like purple; a king is held captive by your tresses. How fair and how pleasant you are, O love, with your delights!

Solomon knew it was vital for him to compliment his bride's body because, as you read in Chapter One, it is evident that it was an area of insecurity for her. This Shulamite was a country girl. She said, "Do not look on me for I am dark." She was tan from working out in the vineyards. And compared with the fair-skinned, pampered ladies of the court, she felt very insecure. So Solomon very wisely built her up in the area where she felt most insecure.

Be sure to compliment parts of their body you know they are insecure about. If your spouse is starved for positive affirmation, and it does not come from you, it opens a door of temptation.

The devil will send someone to give insincere compliments, and if a person is starved for affirmation, they will gravitate towards it. Praise one another lavishly. It is so important!

Affair-Proof Your Relationship with Companionship

Be a companion to your mate, spending time together just enjoying each other's company.

Let look at the Song of Solomon Chapter Seven, Verse 10-13:

I am my beloved's, and his desire is toward me. Come, my beloved, let us go forth to the field; let us lodge in the villages. Let us get up early to the vineyards; let us see if the vine has budded, whether the grape blossoms are open, and the pomegranates are in bloom. There I will give you my love. The mandrakes give off a fragrance, and at our gates are pleasant fruits, all manner, new and old, which I have laid up for you, my beloved.

Notice that Solomon and his bride just hung out together. It was a vital part of their relationship, and so must it be for any thriving marriage. If you have drifted apart, I suggest you each make a list of things you like to do, or things that you might like to try. It could be anything from antique shopping, going to garage sales, taking walks, bicycling, fishing, going to museums, watching football, shopping, gardening, snorkeling, reading, sky diving, cooking, hiking, doing puzzles, learning photography, the list goes on.

"I have a confession to make. My marriage started getting better when I started dating someone even though I was married."

She was an incredible girl. She was beautiful, smart, cunning, strong, and had an immensely strong faith in God. I took her out to dinner, movies, local shows, and always told her how beautiful she was. I can't remember a time when I was mad at her for longer than five minutes. Her smile always seems to brighten up my day no matter the circumstances.

She started leaving work early just so we could have some "alone" time before I had to get back home. I couldn't believe how lucky I was to be dating someone like her even though I was married. I encourage you to try it and see what it can do for your life.

Oh! Did I mention the woman I was dating is my wife? **What did you expect?**

Just because you're married or in a long term relationship doesn't mean your dating life has to end. I needed to continue dating my wife even after I married her. Pursuing your wife shouldn't stop just because you both said, "I do."

Way too often, I see relationships stop growing because people stop taking the initiative to pursue one another. Dating is a time when you get to learn about someone in a special and unique way. Why would you want that to ever stop? Those butterflies you got on the first date shouldn't stop just because the years have passed.

You should wake up each day and pursue your mate as if you are still on your first few dates. You will see a drastic change in your relationship.

When it comes to any relationship, communication and the action of constant pursuit is key. Nobody wants to be with someone who doesn't want to pursue them wholeheartedly. I encourage you to date your spouse, pursue them wholeheartedly, and understand that dating shouldn't end just because you said, "I do." Don't ever forget to have fun together. Set time apart to do at least one activity together every couple of weeks. If you have kids, get a babysitter so it is just the two of you. It will be the best gift you could give your children. If you do not do things together, you will find yourselves drifting apart.

Affair-Proof Your Relationship Through Intimacy

The third way to affair-proof your marriage is by making intimacy a priority.

Let me take you back to the Scripture Song of Solomon 7:10-13:

I am my beloved's, and his desire is toward me. Come, my beloved, let us go forth to the field; let us lodge in the villages. Let us get up early to the vineyards; let us see if the vine has budded, whether the grape blossoms are open, and the pomegranates are in bloom. There I will give you my love. The mandrakes give off a fragrance, and at our gates are pleasant fruits, all manner, new and old, which I have laid up for you, my beloved.

These verses paint a beautiful picture of intimacy between a husband and wife. Couples need to have physical intimacy. In fact, the New Testament commands the husband and wife not to deprive one another except by mutual consent, and then only if they are going to fast and pray.

So how do you create an atmosphere of intimacy? It starts with affirming your spouse. Notice that Solomon has been affirming his wife, complimenting her, and building her up. Now guys, you need to understand that women are wired differently than you. In order for a woman to be intimate, she needs to speak and be spoken to. You have to create an atmosphere for intimacy.

For most men, they just catch a glimpse of their women in the shower and they are ready to go. But for women, it starts differently than that. She is aroused by words, sincere words, and it usually starts around breakfast time. Take time today to create an atmosphere of intimacy. If you do, you will be on your way to experiencing true intimacy.

Check out The Results?

Solomon has been complimenting his wife and affirming her. Look at her response to that affirmation in Song of Solomon 7:10: "I am my beloved's, and his desire is toward me."

She is digging it! She is saying, "He really loves me!" Solomon's affirmation of his bride has created this atmosphere of intimacy. And look what she says next in verse 11: "Come, my beloved, let us go forth to the field; let us lodge in the villages." She is grabbing Solomon's hand and saying, "Let's get a room!" Then there are verses 12-13:

Let us get up early to the vineyards; let us see if the vine has budded, whether the grape blossoms are open, and the pomegranates are in bloom. There I will give you my love. The mandrakes give off a fragrance, and at our gates are pleasant fruits, all manner, new and old, which I have laid up for you, my beloved.

Friends, catch what is going on.

Solomon has affirmed his wife by saying, "Honey, you are beautiful! I am so glad I married you. I married out of my league. You are wonderful. Your body is great. I am so happy!"

Her response? "Wow, he loves me. I'll tell you what, let's go away and have a little love vacation. Let's take a few days off." That is enough to get any husband inspired to rent a hotel room!

If you want to affair-proof your marriage, make intimacy a priority!

Stop It Before It Starts

Most of us say, "It will never happen to me," or "My marriage isn't at risk." But listen to the cold, hard facts: It is estimated that roughly 30-60% of all married individuals in the United States will engage in infidelity at some point during their marriage.

If you think your marriage isn't at risk, or that you'll never be tempted in your marriage, think again. The fact is, we're all at risk.

That is, if we don't take steps to stop an affair before it starts. So just who is susceptible to an affair? Someone who is experiencing:
- Boredom in marriage
- Lack of sexual activity in marriage
- Lack of compliments, validation, and appreciation from their spouse
- Lack of attention from their spouse
- Lack of intimate time in prayer and God's Word

For men and women, adultery begins in the heart. And for men particularly, it begins when the heart is not guarded against what the eyes see and what the mind fantasizes. A woman is more likely to be tempted sexually on an emotional level. There is certainly a physical attraction, but it's usually the accompanying emotional bonding and attachment that leads a woman into an adulterous affair. She is enticed by a man's tenderness, openness, warmth, personality, affection, and attentiveness.

When you sense that someone else is captivating your heart in some way, when this attraction results in increased disappointment or frustration toward your spouse, or when you begin to dwell on or flirt with your fascination, it's time to confront the threat. It's not too late, but it's late enough.

Questions

Are you entertaining any of these common lies and partial truths – or others like them?
- His/her flirting and attention makes me feel good or young again, and it's not hurting anyone.
- We have a connection. He/she really understands me.
- I can talk easily to him/her about everything.

- He/she focuses on me and gives me time to talk.
- There's chemistry between us.
- I can tell he/she is attracted to me.
- I can see myself ending up with him/her.

Stop! You must set a boundary now! You must establish a respectful relational distance between yourself and the man or woman who captures your attention. We're not talking about cutting off all contact with the opposite sex. We're talking about being cautious and alert to temptation in these relationships and maintaining a margin of distance that will help you resist anything that is detrimental to your relationship.

TEN COMMANDMENTS OF LOVE

THE EIGHTH COMMANDMENT OF LOVE:

Be a Person of Integrity

Exodus 20:15 gives us the Eighth Commandment for marriage: "You shall not steal."

Interpretation: Thou Shall Not Take What Does Not Belong To You.

The final three commandants all deal with integrity. To be honest, they really can be grouped together. However, as I examined these three commandments, I discovered some distinct differences. Allow me to elaborate on them.

You may be wondering how stealing applies to a relationship.

Well, you may be surprise to discover how many relationships are affected by this.

Stealing can be done in various forms. Men and women tend to spend money they don't want their mate to know about, whether it's buying another dress or purse you don't need; Purchasing the latest gadget or power tool, going to the club or casino and over spending, or even going online and rerouting items to a friend's house or applying for additional credit cards to hide your spending. All these things can be considered stealing. You see, if you are already or are expecting to get married, there is one thing you need to understand" ALL income is MARITAL income. Simply put, a couple should agree on where and how their money is going to be spent.

Of course every couple should have some level of discretion but that discretion should be budgeted. You should not have to hide what you are spending your money on. You should not have to wait until the person leaves the house to put up what you have purchased.

Why would you steal from yourself?

If you have to hide what you are doing, you are actually stealing from yourself. It does not matter who makes more money. Couples must have a clear understanding about their finances. The worst feeling in the world is when a couple has a financial crisis arise and one party thinks they're OK because "we have something in the savings" only to find out their partner **STOLE IT**. Yes, it is possible to steal your own money!! When you take something that was meant for one purpose and use it for something else, guess what? That's stealing. Many people convince themselves they will replace it, it's not that much, or they won't miss it. However, the reality is, if you can't legitimately justify your spending, then you are nothing more than a thief.

Do you know that 30-40% of marriages end because of finances? In an effort not to be misleading, this statistic includes job loss, previous debt, and other factors. Nevertheless, we can't neglect the fact that money plays a huge role in a relationship. Therefore, knowing how to manage it can make or break it.

Is It Worth It?

Before we move on to the next commandment, let's examine the results of stealing. Let us go back to the financial crises for a moment. Let's say your motor blew in your car. It costs $4,000 to repair it. You say, "No problem that's what the savings is for." You go to the bank to get the money and only $2,000 is there. You thought for sure you had at least $6,000 in the bank. What happened? Unauthorized spending has happened, that's what!!

Now you have to borrow, take from another bill, or use a credit card. Money was already tight, now this puts you in a hole that's going to take a while for you to get out of. Not to mention the tension between that is going to build in the relationship. As a couple you did everything right to make sure you had money to cover reasonable unexpected expenses, but one person did not fulfill their end of the bargain. You try to move pass it but stealing has now added thoughts or concerns regarding trust. If you can't trust your mate, that's another issue. Now this isolated issue of overspending has put a nail in your relationship coffin. If these types of acts continue, it won't be long until you are thinking about separation. Let me ask you a question, is stealing worth losing your relationship?

TEN COMMANDMENTS OF LOVE

THE NINTH COMMANDMENT OF LOVE:

Be Truthful

The Ninth Commandment speaks to the heart of any relationship, "TRUST".
It is found in Exodus 20:16:
"You shall not bear false witness against your neighbor."

Interpretation: Thou Shall Not Lie.

A liar does not make a good partner. Honesty and trust are at the heart of a good relationship. If you take advantage of people for your own gain or speak untruthfully to get ahead, you are not a person to be trusted. And if your mate will lie to someone else, he or she will lie to you as well. Simply put, telling the truth makes you a person of integrity. We've all heard the statement "if you will lie you will steal and if you steal you will kill." This statement simply means that once you fall into a lying trap you will do whatever it takes to get out. If you are always cheating or cutting corners, it will be hard for your partner to trust or respect you.

Your uprightness should make your partner feel proud. Your mate and your family should be able to testify to your integrity. This is really one of the things at the heart of a good relationship. If you are with somebody, and you know they cheat others out of things, it is simply hard to respect that person. You cannot respect someone who does not have integrity. This is a big issue that many people don't think about. But it is vital to a healthy and vibrant marriage because it is hard to fully give yourself to someone who does not have integrity.

There Must Be Trust

I'm a pastor, father, husband, and business owner, and neither my wife nor I have a normal nine to five. We are people on the move. Although we spend a lot of time together, we also spend much of it a part. That means when we are away from each other, we must trust that our partners are not lying about where they are going. If I or my wife had doubts about what the other person was doing, we could not fully concentrate on the assignment at hand. Much of what we do consists of making sure things happen in a certain time frame. That's how we get paid. So lack of trust can literally take food off our table. Therefore, we have learned how to trust each other even when we cannot trace each other.

Recently, I decided to surprise my wife with a romantic dinner. We did not have anything I wanted to cook in the refrigerator, so I had to go shopping. Every week we go over our schedule so we know who's going to do what that week. For example, who's going to pick up the kids, be home for the cleaning service, take care of business concerns, have time for each other, etc. The day before I wanted to cook, I told her I would be back in a little while. Of course she asked me what most spouses would ask me, "Where are you going?" I tried to be as vague as possible. I already knew I was going to have to sneak the groceries in, but now I had to answer this question. I'm so used to just telling her where I'm going, I didn't know how to respond. I must admit that although I was doing something for her, the fact that I could not tell her made me feel slightly uncomfortable. Why? Because our relationship is build on "No Secrets." My wife is one of the few people whom I can trust with anything.

Most people who know me know I can't keep up with anything. At church, my members follow me around just to hand me things I leave behind. At home I'm no different. I'm always misplacing important papers, checks, and even money, but rest assured, my wife always hands these things back to me. Even when members give her blessings for me, she makes sure I receive them. You can't take that kind of trust for granted. She knows if she has a need, she doesn't have to take from me. She knows she has access to everything I have. Even with that knowledge, she does not arbitrarily take things without letting me know. Notice I did not say "without asking for permission." See, it is the simple forms of communication that maintain a healthy relationship.

The Truth Can Set You Free
Truth can be found in various forms.
- Truth about a decision your mate has made
- Truth about where your relationship is going
- Truth about potential temptation

Nothing beats telling the truth. The truth shall set you free!! Relationships that can't handle truth telling will always fall into traps of testing. Holding back the truth can cause permanent damage to a relationship. Nothing should be off-limits in your relationship. That's why you chose your mate, so that you could be open and honest about everything.

If you find that your spouse is holding back, if you feel like he or she does not respect you, take a look inside and see if you are compromising your integrity. Do you cheat on your taxes? Do you tell that "little white lie" to protect yourself or gain an advantage? Do you represent yourself one way, when in fact in your heart you believe something totally different? Are you like the man Solomon speaks of in Proverbs 23:7? *("For as he thinks in his heart, so is he. 'Eat and drink!' he says to you, but his heart is not with you.")* If this is an issue in your life, take it to God today. He will help you become the person of integrity He desires you to be. And when you do, you will find your mate will come to respect you, and as a result, your relationship will be strengthened!

THE TENTH COMMANDMENT OF LOVE:

Be Content with What You Have

We've come to the final commandment for marriage. This commandment is based on the Tenth Commandment given to the nation of Israel in Exodus 20:17,

"You shall not covet your neighbor's house; you shall not covet your neighbor's wife, nor his male servant, nor his female servant, nor his ox, nor his donkey, nor anything that is your neighbor's."

Interpretation: Thou Shall Be Satisfied With What You Have.

This command is very direct. Do not covet. Do not be discontent with what you have. Do not make what you don't have the focus of your life. Accentuate what you do have and what God has blessed you and your spouse with. You do this by celebrating your husband's or wife's strengths and gifting rather than thinking, "Oh, I wish he was this way," or, "I wish she had that."

The Comparison Game
Constant comparison is a relationship killer. If Kim compared me to her previous relationships, our relationship would be in big trouble. Comparison is not just done by comparing previous

relationships, it is done comparing your relationship to that of other couples. The challenge with comparison is that we don't know the whole story. We only know what we see. I have a phrase I usually say in my preaching: "If you want what I have you have to take what I took." I know plenty of couples that would like to have what Kim and I have but they have no idea with that entails. For starters:

- I'm a totally different person now than I was when Kim and I first met.
- We are friends first and lovers second. Many relationships work backwards.
- We have problems just like anybody else.

You see, relationships cannot be manufactured on an assembly line. I believe there are relationship models we can learn from, but no ONE relationship can be duplicated. So don't think about leaving your mate because you've discovered that someone else can do something better. When you get there you may discover that the one thing they do better does not compensate for the ten other things they do worse.

80/20 Rule

Many people call this the **80/20 Rule**. For those who are not familiar with this rule, let me explain. This rule means that a person will consider leaving their partner because of one or two things they don't do well, bypassing the other million things they do wonderfully, leading them to consume the rest of their lives chasing after 20% of what they don't have. Now, I'm no accountant by any stretch of the imagination, but 80% of goodness beats 20% of something, or at worst, 100% of nothing. We must realize that **Nobody is perfect** (not even you)! This means two imperfect people cannot come together to create a perfect relationship. Besides, what's so special about the darned 20%?

Is it Insecurity?

The real reason people chase after the 20% is that *THEY* don't feel fulfilled and good enough in the relationship. Therefore, they have convinced themselves that their partner is the problem. As it turns out, it is our own internal battles that are showing up on the scene and it has absolutely nothing to do with our partner. It's always easier to blame someone else. Sometimes you have to look yourself in the mirror and be satisfied with how you are. Until then, you will never be fully satisfied with your relationship.

Don't Fall for the Fake

That's why pornography and other outside sources should not be invited into your relationship. When influences infiltrate a relationship you can find yourself subconsciously trying to make your situation similar to someone else's. Imagine if people went to bed trying to make the person they are with perform like somebody else. That is a crazy scenario, but that's exactly what you are doing when covet someone else's property. Remember you will always get into trouble if you think the grass is greener on the other side of the fence. Just water your own grass, because on the other side of the fence, it could be Astroturf. Just be who you are, and your relationship will be just the way God intended it to be.

Thank You for Supporting

Nathan E. Austin Ministries

For Additional Books, Speaking Engagements or Workshops

You may contact us at:

954.977.7101

pastora@positioned2prosper.org

www.positioned2prosper.org/neaministries

1525 NW 7th Street

Pompano Beach FL. 33069

www.ingramcontent.com/pod-product-compliance
Lightning Source LLC
Chambersburg PA
CBHW070209100426
42743CB00013B/3110